MY LITTLE GOLDEN BOOK ABOUT

FORMULA ONE RACING

By Stephanie Mulligan • Illustrated by Macky Pamintuan

A GOLDEN BOOK • NEW YORK

Golden Books
An imprint of Random House Children's Books
A division of Penguin Random House LLC
1745 Broadway, New York, NY 10019
penguinrandomhouse.com
rhcbooks.com

Library of Congress Control Number: 2025934228
ISBN 979-8-217-12378-0 (trade) — ISBN 979-8-217-12379-7 (ebook)
Manufactured in the United States of America
10 9 8 7 6 5 4 3 2 1
EU Contact: Penguin Random House Ireland, 32 Nassau Street, Dublin D02 YH68.
https://eu-contact.penguin.ie

Buckle up! It's time to learn all about the daring drivers, magnificent machines, and terrific teams that make up Formula One racing.

Engines are revving, fans are cheering, and drivers are ready. As soon as those five red lights go out, the race is on.

VROOOOM!

The first official Formula One (F1) World Championship race was the British Grand Prix, held in 1950. About 120,000 racing fans, including King George VI, showed up to watch. Now F1 races are seen by millions of viewers, in person and on TV, all around the world.

Why is it called Formula One? Because there's an actual *formula,* or set of rules, to follow. Certain things like the weight of the engine and the width of the tires must be the same for every car built by every F1 team.

These rules change often as teams discover ways to make their cars even better. That's why the cars being raced today look very different than they did in 1950.

Juan Manuel Fangio, a former mechanic from Argentina, was the best F1 driver of the 1950s. He won five championships—a record that would stand for nearly five decades!

Three-time champion Jackie Stewart from Great Britain was the driver to watch in the 1960s and '70s. When he wasn't racing, he was working to make the sport safer for everyone. Thanks to him, seat belts and full-face helmets became mandatory.

Mario Andretti, who moved to the US from Italy when he was a teenager, is America's most successful race car driver. The 1978 Formula One champ had twelve Grand Prix victories during his career. He also competed in other motorsports. He's the only driver to win the Indianapolis 500, the Daytona 500, and the F1 World Championship!

These spectacular races take place on weekends from March to December and are held in countries around the world.

Friday is practice day. Cars are tested, and tire performance is noted. Teams and drivers study the track, or circuit, to get to know all the curves and bumps. In one season, drivers might compete in twenty-four races—and each circuit is different!

One of the most famous F1 circuits is in Monte Carlo at the Monaco Grand Prix. It has the shortest lap—but that doesn't mean it's easy. Extremely narrow streets and remarkably tight corners make it super-challenging.

Alain Prost, nicknamed "the Professor," was a four-time Formula One World Champion from France. He was known for his attention to detail and sharp focus on the track.

Ayrton Senna was a fan favorite from Brazil who made a lasting mark on F1 history. The three-time world champion was especially good at racing in the rain. He was admired for his kindness and generosity as well as his driving talent.

Prost and Senna had a lot of success at Monte Carlo. Between the two of them, they won the Monaco Grand Prix nine times in ten years!

Saturdays on a race weekend begin with more practice time. Teams get to make last-minute tweaks, and drivers test their lap pace before the three qualifying sessions (Q1, Q2, and Q3).

Q1 is an eighteen-minute race. Only a selected number of drivers will make the cut to move on.

Q2 is a fifteen-minute race where, once again, slower drivers are eliminated. The remaining drivers compete in Q3, a twelve-minute race. The driver with the fastest lap during Q3 gets *pole position*. That means they'll start Sunday's race in the very front, or the top of the grid.

Sunday is RACE DAY! Drivers position their cars on the grid based on the results of Saturday's qualifying races—and the Grand Prix begins!

For about two hours, cars race around the track at an average speed of 200 miles per hour (mph) and as fast as 230 mph on a straightaway!

F1 legend Michael Schumacher was the first driver to win seven World Championships. And talk about FAST—the superstar from Germany has a total of seventy-seven fastest laps on record!

Lewis Hamilton holds the record for most pole positions and most Grand Prix wins—he has more than one hundred of each! The brilliant driver from the United Kingdom is considered by many to be the best Formula One driver ever. He won his seventh World Championship in 2020.

What's one of the most important parts of a race? The PIT STOP.

Each driver must stop for at least one tire change. When you stop and how quickly your pit crew works can contribute to whether you win or lose the race.

That's why teams practice pit stops a *lot*!

Don't blink or you might miss it. The pit crew are like magicians—changing all four tires within two to three seconds! Fastest pit stop on record? A blazing 1.8 seconds!

After zooming around the circuit for about 190 miles, the race is over. A black-and-white checkered flag waves until all the cars cross the finish line.

The top three drivers get trophies, and everyone celebrates as it rains confetti.

The top ten drivers score points. At the end of the season, the driver with the most points is the Formula One World Drivers' Champion! That calls for even more confetti!

Max Verstappen is a record-setting driver from the Netherlands. In 2016, at the age of eighteen, he became the youngest winner of a Grand Prix and the first Dutch winner. Five years later, he won his first Drivers' Championship.

The drivers aren't the only ones who can win awards. At the end of a season, the team with the most points earned by their two cars is named Constructors' Champion. Whether it's a chief mechanic or race engineer, everyone on the team has the same goal—bring home a trophy!

Most F1 teams are owned by car manufacturers like Ferrari, McLaren, and Mercedes. Cadillac, the newest team, joined in 2026.

Hundreds of team members work behind the scenes building cars that move so fast they practically fly on the ground. Some of the same techniques that NASA uses to design their rockets are used to design these single-seater, open-wheel cars.

What the drivers wear is just as important as the car they're driving. From head to toe, everything is done with safety in mind. Helmets are custom made to fit each driver. The racing suit is made from fireproof materials and has built-in padding. Grippy gloves provide excellent steering control, especially on rainy days.

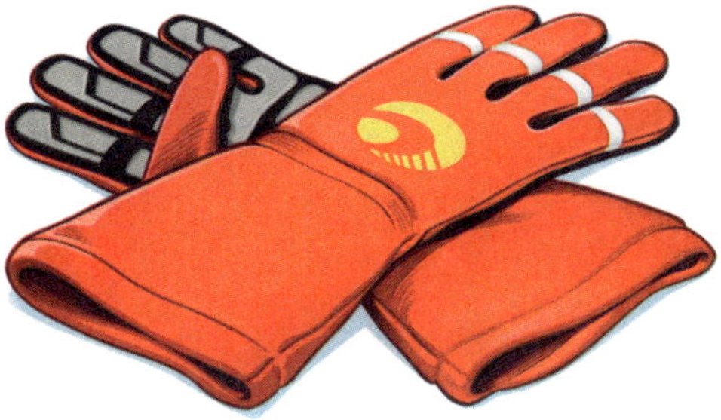

And what about bugs and dirt that get splattered on the front of a driver's helmet? No problem! Helmets come with a bunch of plastic tear-off visors. When one gets dirty, the driver just peels it off.

There have been so many amazing, memorable drivers in the history of F1. And there will always be new champions to look forward to in the future.

F1 Academy, which started in 2023, is a racing series for young women. With the racing experience and the practice time, the hope is that these drivers can gain skills to help them move up the levels of motorsport racing. Maybe all the way to Formula One!

In the world of Formula One racing, teams will continue making cars faster, lighter, and more aerodynamic. Drivers will keep pushing the limits to get the fastest lap possible. And fans will be cheering for their favorites even after the checkered flag is waved.